# Jayaprakash Narayan

## The Eternal Rebel

Varghese K. George

Rupa & Co

Copyright © Rupa & Co 2002
Text © 2002 Varghese K. George

Published in 2002 by

*Rupa & Co*

7/16, Ansari Road, Daryaganj
New Delhi 110 002

*Sales Centres:*
Allahabad Bangalore Chandigarh Chennai
Dehradun Hyderabad Jaipur Kathmandu
Kolkata Ludhiana Mumbai Pune

All rights reserved.
No part of this publication may be reproduced, stored in a retrieval system,
or transmitted in any form or by any means, electronic, mechanical, photocopying,
recording or otherwise, without the prior permission of the publishers.

Cover & Book Design by
Arrt Creations
45 Nehru Apts, Kalkaji, New Delhi 110 019

Printed in India by
Gopsons Paper Ltd
A-14 Sector 60
Noida 201 301

*Jayaprakash Narayan addressing a meeting at Delhi University*

# CONTENTS

**5**
CHAPTER ONE
Making of a Rebel

**18**
CHAPTER TWO
In the Battlefield

**34**
CHAPTER THREE
The Sarvodaya Years

**42**
CHAPTER FOUR
The JP Movement

**54**
CHAPTER FIVE
The Man and His Ideas

**64**
Select Bibliography

CHAPTER ONE

# Making of a Rebel

It was a January evening in Patna. The crowd was formidable. Maulana Abul Kalam Azad and Motilal Nehru's son (Jawaharlal was yet to stand alone) were the speakers. Mesmeric words from two of the greatest orators the Indian subcontinent has ever seen, stirred up the crowd. Among the crowd was a 19-year-old student, who had taken a break from his hectic preparations for the Intermediate exams just weeks away. Students should leave schools; lawyers should leave courts and civil servants their jobs — the speakers exhorted the crowd. The year was 1921. The Non-Cooperation Movement against British rule in India had begun.

It had been brewing for a while. Two years had passed since the killing of 379 unarmed civilians on April 13, 1919 at Jallianwalla Bagh, but the wound on India's psyche was still fresh. British brutality had been on the rise. Peasants, labourers and professionals were aggrieved. Seething collective anger finally led Indians to revolt against their imperialist masters in the first Non-Cooperation Movement. Dormant anti-imperialism sprung into action at a national scale. Mahatma Gandhi had fully taken command of the infant struggle, marking the beginning of the new phase of the freedom struggle.

The 19-year-old student at the Patna meeting went back home and declared his studies stopped, in response to the call made by the Congress. His name was Jayaprakash Narayan. When an embittered nation struggled against foreign rule, a sense of duty captivated the young student who had been exposed to tales of foreign misrule and sufferings of the poor even before he

*JP's Mother, Phool Rani Devi*

had heard speeches of Azad and Jawaharlal. For a family that had built castles of hope around their brilliant eldest son, Jayaprakash's decision was shattering. For Jayaprakash, as always in his life, his decisions were his alone and not negotiable.

Until he finished primary schooling, he stayed in his home village, Sitabdiara, 50 miles away from Patna. Sitabdiara was on the confluence of the Ganga and Ghagra rivers on Bihar's border with what was then United Province and is now Uttar Pradesh. As the rivers often changed courses, this village shifted between the two states. In this, as in all villages, people lived in settlements seggregated along caste lines. Kayasthas, the caste that Jayaprakash was born into, lived in Lala Tola. Traditionally the Kayasthas had taken to government service quite early.

Harsu Dayal, Jayaprakash's father, was a revenue official in Bihar's Canal Department. Phool Rani Devi was his mother. Jayaprakash was born on October 11, 1902, the third child in the family. Those were times when cholera and plague killed people in hordes and Hari Prakash, Harsu Dayal's eldest son had died of cholera at the age of thirteen. Chandramukhi, his eldest daughter died of the plague. The next four siblings survived — Chandravati, Jayaprakash, Chandrakala and Rajeshwar. Phool Rani perpetually feared that she would lose Jayaprakash too to death. She became overly protective about him — Jayaprakash was not allowed to move around too much with his peers, not allowed to swim or ride. He withdrew himself to his own world, talked very little and always appeared to be in deep thought. "He behaves too old for his age," Harsu Dayal often told his wife. He even talked late, making his parents anxious. By the time Rajeshwar was born, Phool Rani was more relaxed. The contrast between the brothers was stark — Jayaprakash an introvert and an endless meditator; Rajeshwar a chirpy, loud socialiser. His parents thought he was a little too "girlish." In his loneliness, Jayaprakash sought company in pets. He got terribly upset seeing others' sufferings. The compassionate young child once saved the job of his incompetent tutor who was about to be sacked by Harsu Dayal.

*JP's father, Harsu Dayal*

*Bankim Chandra Chatterjee*

Kayasthas were an educated lot. Even Babu Nandan Lal, Jayaprakash's grandfather who was a police inspector, spoke English. The family subscribed to the *Anand Bazar Patrika* and through it Jayaprakash peeped into the world outside, where protest against foreign rule was fermenting. At the age of ten, Jayaprakash took to the world of words — he started with reading about the mythological heroes and soon laid his hands on Bankim Chandra Chatterjee. Then he moved on to national heroes of foreign countries — like Garibaldi and Valera. He read the *Gita* and about Gandhi who had just come to India with his ideas of non-cooperation and *satyagraha* conceived in South Africa, and was soon to try it in Champaran in the year of 1917.

Jayaprakash moved to Patna for higher studies in 1915, at the age of thirteen. Saraswati Bhawan, the hostel of Patna Collegiate School was already a haven of nationalists. The hostel then had a battery of students who would later be leaders of the freedom struggle. *Ahimsa* and *satyagraha* had not caught the imagination of the nation then. Protests against the British were largely localised and often led to armed uprisings. Chotan Singh, a companion, introduced Jayaprakash to a revolutionary youth from Bengal and a pamphlet titled *Desh ki Batein* — facts about the nation. It talked about imperialism and how the British rule was draining India economically. "Bengal is ready for revolution. Now it's the turn of Bihar," the anonymous revolutionary assured Jayaprakash. Wide-eyed, Jayaprakash listened to revolutionary exploits in Bengal. One night, by the Ganges, the threesome held their fingers to a candle flame and committed their life to the cause of revolution. This initiation by fire left a long lasting impression on JP's mind, but soon after that night of devotion, Chotan Singh disappeared and never returned. But the fire inside Jayaprakash still burnt, and for decades to come, he was convinced that an armed rebellion was the only way to get the British out.

*JP's ancestral home at Sitabdiara*

Meanwhile, Jayaprakash's eldest sister Chandravati got married to Braj Bihari Sahay, who was based in Patna. Jayaprakash moved in with his sister and brother-in-law. He was a hardworking student who would forget to eat while tackling a mathematical puzzle. He was equally ferocious about his rights from then on. He protested against scheduling an exam on the day of *puja,* by bunking it — his first lesson in protest that earned him a few whips from the English headmaster.

At that time, Rajendra Prasad, India's future president was the fulcrum of nationalist activities in Bihar. It was with a relative, Shambu Sharan, that Jayaprakash went to Prasad's house first. Braj Kishore Babu, who brought Gandhi to Champaran earlier was present there. In Jayaprakash, Braj Kishore found a good match for his daughter Prabhavati. Bright and hardworking, Jayaprakash was a promising young man. In 1919, when Jayaprakash was eighteen and Prabhavati fourteen, they were married. Through his marriage, Jayaprakash gained access to the powerful circuit of national leaders; by 1922, Braj Kishore, close to Gandhiji, took over as the Bihar president of the Congress. With his superb intellect and solid commitment, Jayaprakash too proved worthy of their company. Those days, custom demanded that young couples stayed separated for a stipulated time even after marriage.

*JP as a student in the United States*

*JP's wife, Prabhavati Devi*

Prahba continued to stay at her home and Jayaprakash continued with his studies.

For intermediary studies, he won a scholarship of fifteen rupees a month and took science as his optional subject. As the exams neared, he worked harder but then Jawaharlal's speech interrupted him. The day after Azad and Nehru spoke, thousands of students marched to Rajendra Prasad's house dedicating themselves to the cause of anti-imperialism. For Jayaprakash, even his appearance changed; from a cap, shirt, coat and English shoes, he slipped into rough *khadi*.

The Non-Cooperation Movement flared-up. But when 22 policemen were killed at Chauri Chaura by an irate mob, Gandhi suspended the Non-Coperation Movement in April 1922. Jayaprakash was unwilling to join any government funded educational institution so Braj Kishore suggested he go to England and continue his studies. "I found it ironic — boycotting English-run schools here and going to England! I decided to go to the United States," Jayaprakash recalled later.

Nobody approved of Jayaprakash's move, though Prabhavati, true to the role of a traditional wife, did not oppose her husband's wishes. On August 16 1922, Jayaprakash sailed for US, ignoring everyone's protest. With the Rs 2000 he had earned as wedding gift from his in-laws and other contributions from his father, Jayaprakash had $ 600 with him while leaving. The voyage to the US itself was symbolic of the tempestuous life that he himself chose later in life — the cargo boat carrying him almost succumbed to a typhoon in South China sea, en-route to Kobe. A sea-sick and lonely JP had to keep to himself partly because he was a sworn vegetarian and partly because he was too shy and introverted. In Japan, he stayed for a month and then set on an 18-day voyage to the U.S. On October 8, 1922, JP reached San Francisco, which fascinated him because, he was told, there he could, "work and study."

He did both. The term at the University of California was to start three months later. Jayaprakash joined a ranch as a grape-picker. Working eight hours, he earned eight dollars a day. After one semester at California, he moved to the University of Iowa where tuition fee was less. From there he went to Chicago and then to Wisconsin. At Wisconsin, he met the American Communist Abraham Landy who introduced him to the Indian Communist M.N. Roy's writings. In Marxism, Jayaprakash found the theoretical root for his passionate convictions about social realities. When Landy earned a faculty position at Ohio, Jayaprakash too followed him. That was Jayaprakash's last stint in the US as a student. By this time, the student who went to study chemical engineering had switched to sociology; his dissertation "Societal Variation" explored the ways

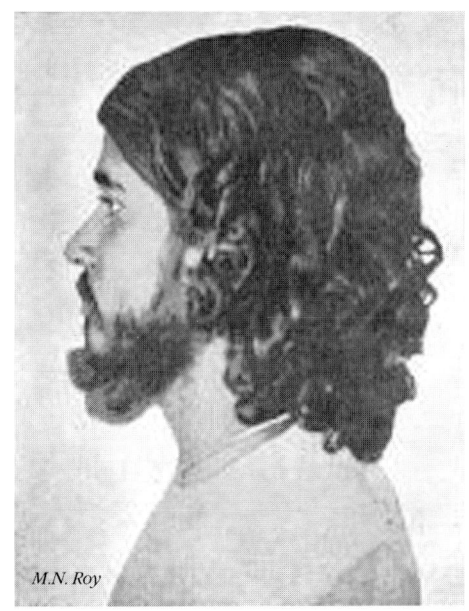

*M.N. Roy*

and reasons of social change, of course, from a Marxist perspective. His knack for mathematics never died, but he added more areas of interests to it — history, psychology, economics and literature. "His whole outlook is based on a desire to know how to do to something to help society," a professor of his commented. Another professor found in Jayaprakash "germs of leadership" and "aggressiveness of thought."

In the US, JP worked in mines, in slaughter houses, factories and ranches. Sometimes also as a shoeshine boy and as a cleaner in a hotel. In the summer of 1926, he sold hair-straighteners and fairness creams to the blacks in the suburbs of Chicago. "Manufacturers preferred Indian students, because

*With a friend in America*

we could tell them, "Look at our hair. Look how light our complexion is. This was cheating. But I don't think I did the cheating part," he recalled years later. But the winter of 1926 was extremely difficult and Jayaprakash fell ill. Treatment by a cheap quack nearly killed him. Bed-ridden for three months, he cabled home for financial help. Harsu Dayal mortgaged his property and sent $ 900 that saved Jayaprakash's life. Severely malnourished, he gave up his strict vegetarianism and ate meat on doctor's advice. After graduation, he got a scholarship and three months later an assistantship at Ohio. With an assured earning of $ 80 a month, Jayaprakash felt secure.

Gandhi had suggested even before her marriage that Prabhavati join him at the Wardha Ashram; with Jayaprakash gone to the US, Prabhavati accepted the suggestion and went to Wardha. While Prabhavati was being baptised by the moralistic ideals of Gandhi, across the oceans, Jayaprakash found his faith in Marxism and dialectical materialism.

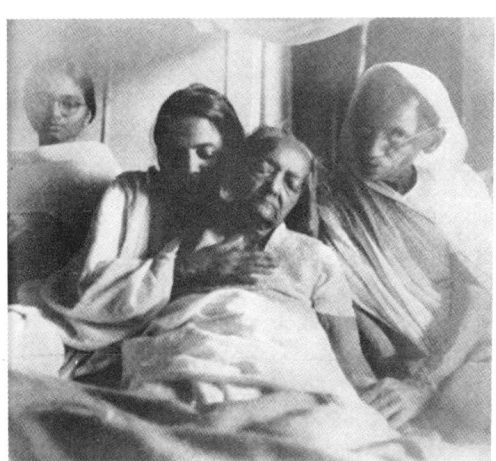

*Kasturba Gandhi, at her death-bed*

Jayaprakash had remained committed to Prabhavati in America where opportunities for a fling were not far from the handsome charmer — in fact, he once barely overcame a sexual temptation. Prabhavati was a significant presence in Gandhi's ashram, though she was not to become as famous as Gandhi's other female disciples. She led the morning prayers at the ashram and later Kasturba died in her arms in the Agha Khan's Palace in Pune in 1943. In April 1929, barely months before Jayaprakash's return, Prabha wrote to him that she wanted to observe *brahmacharya* — as Gandhi himself and many of his disciples had already decided. What did he think? Prabha asked Jayaprakash. The significance of her suggestion did not strike Jayaprakash until Gandhi bluntly wrote to him; "If you want to marry again, you may do so." "I will accept whatever you decide," Jayaprakash replied to Prabhavati.

It was time to leave the US. Seven years of living in the mecca of capitalism had turned Jayaprakash into a votary of socialism. For JP, the world's salvation rested in Marxism. For years he clung to his beliefs — at times, with the obstinacy of child. He witnessed from close quarters, the affluence of the few and the misery of the exploited. Writings of the Indian communists that linked imperialism and capitalism fired the

*JP with wife, Prabhavati Devi*

*JP with Yusuf Meherally and Subhas Chandra Bose*

nationalist sentiment in Jayaprakash. Success stories of the newly founded socialist USSR inspired and offered him the view of the world that he wanted to build. Jayaprakash wanted to go to the USSR. "But the struggle against imperialism is in India, not in the USSR," his father-in-law wrote to him and Jayaprakash sailed for India.

Jayaprakash's roots were firm. As he touched the Indian shore, Jayapraksh changed to his *desi dhoti* and *kurta*. Reaching home, he touched the feet of elders. Prabhavati had come to Patna to receive him. Meanwhile, at Wardha, a new storm of popular resistance against the British was being conceived. After the mass education programmes through the 1920s, Gandhi was gradually convinced that the nation had overcome the beastly urge displayed at Chauri Chaura. The country awoke with a new mission and a new slogan. Within weeks after Jayaprakash's return at the Lahore Session of 1929, Congress declared *Purna Swaraj* as its goal.

*Jayaprakash Narayan*

CHAPTER TWO

# In the Battlefield

From the doorway of his ground floor room at Wardha Ashram, where he had gone with his wife, Jayaprakash watched stalwarts of the national movement climbing down the stairs after concluding the Congress Working Committee meeting. JP (Jayaprakash had gained this alias during his American stay) was trying to spot Gandhi. Suddenly someone whose face had been familiar walked upto JP and said, "*Mein Jawaharlal hoon.*" Nehru had learnt about the return of a young nationalist from the US. The two hit it off well since they shared the same worldview, including their criticism of Gandhi's economic and social thinking and saw Indian issues from an international perspective.

Prabhavati had brought JP to Wardha with the intention of converting him to Gandhian ideals and Gandhi received him warmly. JP was unsure about his future plans in November 1929 when he reached India. After spending a day with Prabha in Patna he went to visit his ailing

*Mahatma Gandhi*

mother and father at Sitabdiara where people had organised a grand felicitation for him, complete with traditional musicians and performers and even a *shuddhi puja* to absolve him of the sin of having crossed the seas. After a few days, he joined Prabha in Patna and then travelled to Wardha. Gandhi did not impress the Marxist. The spinning wheel, *pujas* and prayers and the overall spiritualism at the ashram generally made him angry with Gandhi, who JP thought was a "reactionary". Gandhi, who had encouraged Prabha to read about socialism, that being her husband's ideology, was not in a hurry. "One day, this man will talk my language," Gandhi prophesised and it came true though Gandhi was dead by then.

REJOICE and be exceeding GLAD: FOR SO PERSECUTED they the prophets which were BEFORE YOU...

*A cartoon by O V Vijayan*

Fascimile of JP's letter to Gandhi

Towards the end of December 1929, JP and Prabha travelled with Gandhi to Lahore to attend the All India Congress Committee (AICC) session there. On December 31 and January 1, 1930 the AICC met and elected Jawaharlal Nehru as the president. The Indian flag — red, white, green; red later replaced by saffron — was hoisted. The Indian National Congress was declared India's legal government and January 26, 1930, was celebrated across the nation as Independence Day. Thus began the Civil Disobedience Movement, of which the most reverberating moment was the Salt Satyagraha later that year.

By the end of the Lahore Session, JP asked Prabha about her plans — whether she planned to go back to Wardha or accompany him. On consulted by Prabha, Gandhi told her that it was her "duty to go with her husband." Nehru offered JP a job worth Rs 150 a month, as secretary of the labour research bureau of the AICC, at Allahabad. Both JP and Prabhavati first stayed in rented accommodation in Allahabad and then moved into Swaraj Bhavan, Nehru's ancestral house, when the Nehrus moved to their new house, Anand Bhawan. JP's closeness with Nehru grew fast — Nehru called him Jayaprakash and JP called him Nehru Bhai. Slightly away from the scurry of political activities, Kamala, Nehru's wife, poured out her lonely heart to Prabhavati. JP and Prabha developed a fondness for Indira, Nehru's daughter of thirteen years, who he held responsible for many a sin decades later, when she was the prime minister and he, the crusader.

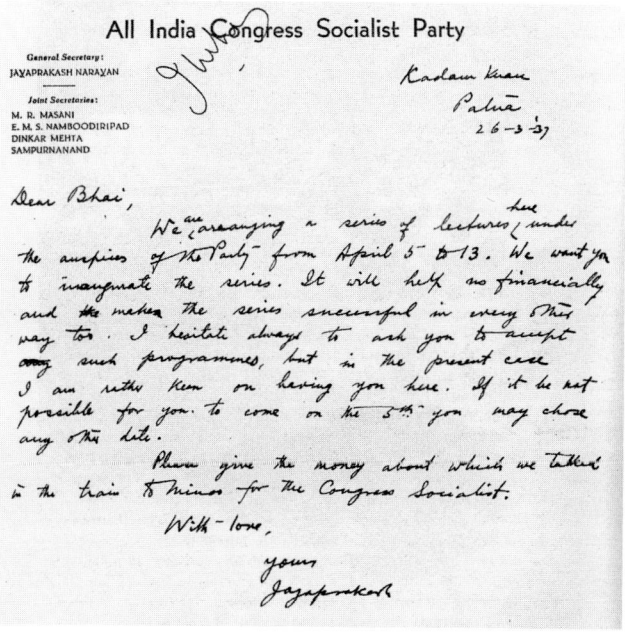

Fascimile of JP's letter to Jawaharlal Nehru

JP's mother was seriously ill and battling for her life. Political commitment and family expectations pulled JP in different directions. Gandhi advised him to be a good son first, since he would have opportunity to serve the country later on too. His mother died and JP found that his father was in deep debt, acquired to finance Jayaprakash in the US. He wanted a better-paid job. Gandhi then asked G.D. Birla, who appointed JP as his secretary. JP found the

*JP as General Secretary, C.S.P., c. 1935*

job too suffocating and soon left that and went back to Allahabad on Nehru's insistence.

All senior leaders were arrested during the Civil Disobedience Movement. While JP and Nehru were travelling together to Bombay, Nehru was arrested. With senior leaders in jail, responsibility fell on JP's shoulders to carry on the Movement. JP travelled three times, across the length and breadth of the country to keep the reserve structure of the Congress organisation alive. On September 7, 1932, JP was in Madras, accompanying a British Labour Party delegation. JP thought the police would not pick him from among a British delegation. It was a wrong calculation, and JP landed in the Nasik jail in Bombay.

Nasik jail, where he met the future Socialist leaders — Asoka Mehta, Minoo Masani, Achyut Patwardhan, and N.G. Goray — marked another beginning in his political life. They all agreed that socialism was their aim, though each one perceived it differently and were sceptical of Gandhian methods. After his release from the jail, JP spent time in organising relief for the victims of an earthquake in Bihar on January 15, 1934. On May 17, 1934 with Marxist theoretician Narendra Dev as chairman, the Congress Socialist Party (CSP) was launched — it was a party within the Congress party. In *Congress Socialist*, the mouthpiece of the Socialist wing, JP sarcastically wrote of Gandhi,

*JP with Swami Sahajanand Saraswati and other Kisan leaders*

"How shall we learn that imperialism cannot be overthrown by the manufacture of salt or picketing of liquor shops? From experience — our own and of others."

Unlike Gandhi who always moved cautiously and made short-term demands with the British — he wrote that the Lahore "independent resolution need frighten nobody" — JP and his Socialist colleagues were very clear that complete withdrawal of the British was their political

*Fascimile of JP's letter to Nabakrushna Chaudhuri*

agenda. While Nehru took over as the AICC president again in 1936, he was happy to have the Socialist crowd around him, since they confirmed with Nehru ideologically and were a counterweight to the Right within the party. JP was nominated to the Congress Working Committee, but when the Congress decided to participate in the Interim Government of 1936, JP resigned from his seat in protest.

Around this time, JP was also frustrated that the Congress was not taking up questions of social and economic reforms. During the period of 1933-36, JP worked on *Why Socialism,* his first treatise that explained the objective of the CSP. He explained, to establish socialism, state power is necessary and how to acquire that power was irrelevant. "Socialism has a single form, and a single principle and that is Marxism," JP wrote. He dedicated himself to organising *kisan sabhas* and *mazdoor sanghs* since he believed only peasant and labour organisations could

*With P.C. Joshi after the Faizpur session in the thirties*

end imperialism and bring about socialism. He criss-crossed the country with this message and was largely successful in getting these sections to join the Congress in large numbers.

Though an unflinching believer in Marxism, JP was a critic of Indian Communists because in their analysis, the Indian national movement was bourgeoisie. JP did not agree. For him, national freedom was a pre-requisite to the larger aim of socialism. However, Jayaprakash nurtured the dream of forging Marxist unity. In 1936, he invited CPI activists to join the CSP and the invitation was accepted because the Communists International had already directed it to join hands with "bourgeois democrats" in order to resist the emerging threat of fascism in the world. The Communists very quickly took over control of the CSP and within a few years, split it to regroup as CPI again. Jayaprakash personally felt cheated. This incident, coupled with the abrupt withdrawal of the Communists from the Quit India Movement in 1942 on the grounds that Britain and the USSR were allies in a "people's war" against German fascism, left a deep distrust in JP's mind of Communists which was never rectified. Later on in his life, JP would ally with the political Right but never with the Left.

JP's criticism against the British war efforts resulted in his arrest under charges of sedition in early 1940. In the court, JP pleaded guilty of the charges. "As an Indian, it is my duty to

*After a CSP meeting in Assam*

liberate my country as it is the duty of the British to defend his in the war" he told the court. JP was sentenced for nine months in the Hazaribagh jail and, on release, went to Bombay. Police got wind of his "underground plans," and he was back in jail almost as soon as he got out. This time under the Defence of India rules, it was a preventive arrest that did not require trial.

In 1940-41, thirty thousand Congressmen were arrested. The political scene in the country was simmering again. Britain was at war against Germany. Socialists were of the opinion that the Congress should make use of this opportunity and organise a mass uprising within the country.

JP spent his first few days in Bombay's Arthur Road Prison and then he was shifted to the Deoli Jail near Ajmer. JP tried to smuggle out a message in which he exhorted socialist cadres to prepare for an armed assault against the British, but the message was confiscated. British officials leaked the letter with the intention of creating a rift between JP and Gandhi, who disapproved of violent methods. Gandhi did not take the bait. "To practice deception, to resort to secret methods and even to plot murder are all honourable (in Western warfare) and turn perpetrators into national heroes," said Gandhi. Later, when JP escaped from jail, Gandhi said that too was fine, "since JP did not believe in non-violence anyway."

*Fascimile of JP's letter to Rammanohar Lohia*

JP escaped from jail in Hazaribagh, where he was shifted from Deoli. Conditions in the Deoli Jail were subhuman and JP protested along with other prisoners. He went on fast that lasted

*After coming out of Agra Jail in 1946*

for 31 days. Once the issue grew big, the colonial government closed down the jail, and JP was shifted. On August 8, 1942, the very day when the AICC resolved to make the British "Quit India," JP walked into the Hazaribagh jail.

It was the Diwali day — 9 November, 1942. Most of the Hindu warders were on leave and the jail itself was in a festive mood. An accomplice of JP and his gang entertained the inmates with stories. JP and six others had done their ground work — they realised the sentry on rounds returned to a point in every eight minutes, meaning within eight minutes the jail-break operation

*In Patna, after release from jail, April 1946*

had to be finished. The group got into action the moment, the sentry crossed the particular point they had chosen to scale the wall. They climbed on *dhotis* tied to each other and hooked atop the wall. In six minutes they were all across the wall and running for their life. A run that was made difficult by the fact that they left behind the bag containing extra clothes, some money and most important of all in the unfriendly forest terrain of Hazaribagh, shoes. The British put a price tag of Rs 5000 on JP's head, and a few months later increased to Rs 10,000 — that was equivalent to a labourer's salary for a good 30 years!

The jailbreak made JP into a folk hero in contemporary nationalist chronicles. JP's letters to

*JP with members of the National Executive of the C.S.P. From left to right: Yusuf Meherally, Achyut Patwardhan, Rammanohar Lohia, S. Sajjed Zaheer, Asoka Mehta, Narendra Deva, S.M. Joshi, Kamaladevi Chatopadhyay, Mubarak Saghar, JP, M.R. Masani and S.S. Batlivala*

"all freedom fighters," which was an analyis of anti-imperialist struggle, signed from "somewhere in India," created a sensation. JP reached Delhi and in a meeting with his other colleagues decided to raise a freedom brigade. He took up this responsibility and left for Nepal to be out of reach of the police. Meanwhile large-scale uprisings were being reported from all over the country.

In Nepal, he was discovered but managed to escape narrowly, in May 1944. In September, the same year JP decided to go to the North West Frontier Province and organise the Pathans into revolt. By this time, JP had become a major embarrassment to the British government, which was unable to apprehend him. JP boarded the Frontier Mail with a surname Mehta and felt safe. Midway, an army officer in civilian dress entered his compartment and asked, "Are you Jayaprakash Narayan?" JP protested, but to no avail. He was arrested and taken to Lahore Fort where he was tortured for days to extract information about the underground movement. JP's arrest and torture became a national issue. He was then moved to Agra Central Jail. When he was released from there on April 11, 1946, he had become hugely popular, only next to Gandhi and Nehru.

The Quit India Movement was bearing fruit. At the June 14-15, 1947 session of the AICC, called to discuss the Mountbatten Plan, JP and Lohia fought with Nehru and Patel on the issue of allowing Mountbatten to partition the country. Till the last moment, JP tried to persuade Gandhi to resist partition actively. But Gandhi was helpless. JP felt serious doubts about continuing with the Congress party. On January 29, 1948, a day before Gandhi was shot, JP, met him and said that Socialists could not remain within the Congress. Later he criticised Home Minister Sardar Patel for inadequate security provided to Gandhi. Patel who never quite liked the socialism of JP wanted socialists out of the party. In 1948, at a conference in Nasik on March 19-21, they decided to leave the Congress. "I am conscious that when we leave the Congress we shall leave behind many friends and valued comrades with whom our bonds of personal and ideological attachment should never snap." JP concluded his Congress days. Nehru was certainly foremost among these valued comrades.

The Socialist's attempts to explore an alternative to the Congress proved futile. Under the huge banyan tree called Nehru, nothing else found roots. The first general election of 1952 wiped out the Socialists and all other opposition parties in the country. Ramanandan Mishra, JP's comrade from the night when they escaped from the Hazaribagh prison, held JP responsible

*With Prabhavati during the three-week self-purificatory fast in Pune*

for the debacle, since JP was friendly with Nehru. JP cried like a child hearing this. Awed by the intrigues of party politics and realising his inability to manage the show in a highly complex political atmosphere, JP went into a bout of soul searching.

Atrocities of Stalinist USSR were also a rude shock to JP. He had already begun pondering over his convictions. Could there be a better way of achieving social good, he asked himself. And the result began showing — the man who used to ridicule Gandhi for wasting time in spinning, took to the *charkha*. The man who looked the other way when his wife Prabhavati went for the morning prayers now joined her.

JP's definite break with Marxism came in 1952. He had negotiated a postal and telegraphic employee's strike with Communications Minister Rafi Ahmad Kidwai. The minister backed out of a certain assurance, in effect, duping the employees. JP thought it was his duty as a leader to ensure that the commitment to the employees was honoured. From June 23, 1952, JP embarked on a 21-day strike at Pune's Dinshah Mehta Clinic to purify himself, and as a self-penance since he found himself "guilty of carelessness and negligence." Towards the end of the fast, JP wrote an article *Incentives to Goodness*. In a remarkable paragraph that demonstrates JP's facility with the language he wrote, "For many years, I have worshipped at the shrine of the goddess dialectical materialism — which seemed to me intellectually more satisfying than any other philosophy. ... In a material civilisation, man has no rational incentive to be good. It may be that in the kingdom of dialectical materialism, fear makes men conform, and the party takes the place of God. But when God himself turns vicious, to be vicious becomes an universal code. ... I feel further that the task of social reconstruction cannot succeed under the inspiration of a materialist philosophy."

From materialism to spiritualism, from party politics to social work and from coerced social reform to the conversion of the minds, JP metamorphosed his philosophy. The Sarvodaya Movement was his next stopover. And it was not his last.

CHAPTER THREE

# The Sarvodaya Years

In his new avatar JP was convinced of the futility of violence as a means of social change. What was required was the reform of the society, by persuading every individual to the path of socialism. Changing institutions alone would not do; the individual should change. In his speeches through the 1950's, JP dissected the failures of socialist experiments elsewhere and sought an Indian variation of that, which he finally discovered in Vinoba Bhave's Sarvodaya-Bhudan Movements. Vinoba was hailed as Gandhi's spiritual heir those days. Jayaprakash whom Gandhi called the greatest socialist in India, was to be soon known as the greatest Gandhian.

Jayaprakash's shift to Gandhism and his disenchantment with the socialist experiment were simultaneous and gradual. Nehru wanted JP to join his cabinet after the 1952 elections; JP set 14 conditions — that included nationalisation of banks and stopping of privy-purse to erstwhile princes — for doing so. Nehru replied that socialist measures at such fast pace could be dangerous and JP did not join the cabinet. JP continued to criticise Nehru for his perceived inadequate commitment to socialism. Even after his 1952 rejection of Marxism, he continued nurturing ambitions of unifying socialists who where by now scattered and at loggerheads with each other. In 1957, a disillusioned JP bade good-bye to party politics completely.

Vinoba had innovated the concept of Bhudan in 1951 while touring the Telengana region in Andhra Pradesh where peasants inspired by Marxism had begun killing their exploitative landlords. "What does *ahimsa* mean to us who are starving while the landlords live in affluence off our labour," a landless peasant confronted Vinoba in the village Pochampalli.

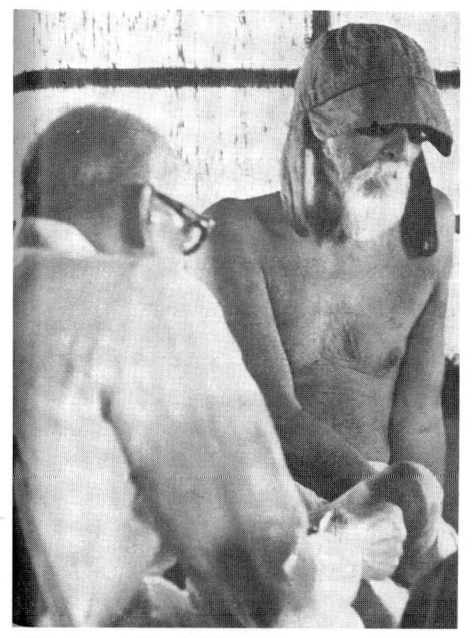

*With his guru, Vinoba Bhave in August 1974*

Vinoba persuaded the landlords in the village to donate 80 acres of land for its landless people. That was the beginning of the *Bhudan* (land gift) Movement. In the Telengana region alone Vinoba collected 12,000 acres of land. In September and November, he walked to Delhi collecting another 20,000 acres. *Sarvodaya* (upliftment of all) was meant as a non-exploitative social and economical structure and as an alternate to all other radical political philosophies. One could commit to different types of *dans* (gifts) of wealth, land, life or effort. Congress governments, both at the Centre and the States offered support to the Movement, since all feared a massive uprising among the landless. Voluntary

*With Prabhavati, after Independence*

donations emphasised by the Sarvodaya Movement in contrast to legislative measures to address the question of land reforms was a please-all solution. Vinoba's message spread quickly and the Bhudan Movement appeared set to become India's indigenous social revolution.

JP was impressed. In his socialist meetings, he suggested that they seek lessons in Vinoba's spiritual regeneration, considering the fact that their scientific socialism was not catching up. In August 1951 and in June 1952, just before his landmark fast, he met Vinoba twice and wrote that he met "a group who are in far greater touch with the people and their problems than any other group in the country." Soon enough JP donated half of his 50 acres of land. In

April 1954, at the Sixth Sarvodaya Conference in Gaya, Bihar, in the presence of Nehru, Dr Radhakrishnan, Dr Rajendra Prasad, and Acharya Kripalini, JP said he was turning a *jeevandani* (one who has gifted his life) for Sarvodaya. He retired from party politics. "The decision that I took was not made on the spur of the moment. I was being slowly driven towards it for months past," JP wrote later.

*Acharya Kripalini*

The Bhudan Movement went well in the 1950s and then slowed down. In the first decade, pledges of nearly a million acres of land were collected. JP had made villages the focal point of his activities. JP dreamed of building village self-government (*gramswarajya*) by collective control of productions devices and collective decision-making. To test his dream, he founded an *ashram* at Sukhodeora in Gaya. Along with a hundred followers, JP tried to establish a model of community living there. By introducing rainwater harvesting and improvising crude village technologies and irrigation JP tried to make a self-contained community there. JP theorised that "party-less democracy," in which villagers directly controlled their destiny was the ideal political system for India. While Nehru introduced the Panchayati Raj in the First Five-Year Plan, JP advised Sarvodaya workers to participate in it, but soon got disillusioned with that. JP believed that the macro policies of the government were detached from the realities of the villages and often got into arguments with Nehru, who consulted JP on such issues. But the distance between the two was growing, with Nehru once accusing JP of "playing hide and seek between politics and the Bhudan Movement."

"He will be the prime minister of India," Nehru had said of Jayaprakash in 1948. While Nehru was failing in health by 1962, the question of who after Nehru came up and JP's name figured

*Jayaprakash Narayan with Prime Minister Nehru at the National Integration Conference in New Delhi, October 1961*

prominently. There was nobody as popular as JP though he was not part of a political party. Some remarks from JP himself reinforced speculations that he was interested in the top slot. Interested or not, JP did not become the prime minister after Nehru.

It was not merely over economic policies that JP confronted the Nehru government. Foreign policy, a holy cow even today, became the subject of JP's criticism. He said the Indian stand on Hungary's invasion by USSR in 1956 was "double standards" and chided the government on its Tibetan policy in 1959. Most blasphemous of all, he argued in favour of better relations with Pakistan and talks to resolve the Kashmir problem. In 1964, he tried to negotiate a settlement with the Naga tribes, which revolted against the Indian government. His causes were far-flung: "peace marchers in Northern Rhodesia, political prisoners in Indonesia, panchayats in Nepal, police firing in Patna, nuclear tests in the Pacific, co-operatives in Uttar Pradesh and above all, the salvation of the mankind," writes Welles Hangen in his book *After Nehru, Who?* JP travelled within the country and abroad spreading the message of Bhudan, lecturing on the unique experiment underway in India. Meanwhile, in the 1960s, Vinoba and JP founded Tarun Shanti Sena, a brigade of volunteers to intervene and prevent communal clashes.

By the mid-1960s, the Bhudan Movement was revealing its limitations. Most of the land donated was found to be low yielding and in many cases barren. Not even one fifth of the land collected was distributed among the landless. In most cases, the pledge to gift land remained only that — pledges — and the original owners continued cultivating it. Nearly 5500 villages of Bihar that were committed to *gramdan,* a higher form of *bhudan,* where the entire village land was to be given under collective ownership and management reverted to its earlier status. In 1968, JP tried to mobilise support for *Bihardan,* but the movement had begun fading already.

Still, the last episodes of the Sarvodaya Movement triggered another churning in JP's intellectual evolution. In 1970, JP was recovering from illness at a small station Pauri in Garhwal, where he received the message that Naxalites in Muzaffarpur had threatened to kill two Sarvodaya volunteers. Naxalites (Marxists who believed in armed class struggle and derived their name from the place Naxalbari in West Bengal where they first organised a revolt) believed that movements like the Sarvodaya were diversionary tactics that pardoned exploitation. JP and Prabhavati reached Musehari Block in the district on June 3 and stayed there for months at a stretch, going from house to house. Villagers were living in fear of Naxalite attacks and JP's presence gave courage to them. JP addressed villagers in small groups and sometimes individually. In the beginning, it was a difficult task since the villagers were sceptical and often confused about JP's concept of non-violent revolution and village government. With the efforts of several months, JP and his team managed to convince a large section of the villages that "Naxalites were the product of a system and the remedy is to change that system." JP considered Naxalism "primarily a social, economic, political and administrative problem and only secondarily a law and order problem." But his intensive interaction with the villagers for an indefinite period of time gave him new insights. "I had not buried myself in this manner before in a limited rural area for such highly intensive work. ... I must confess that the socio-

*With Shanker Rao Deo at the Bihar Bhudan March*

economic reality in the village, on close examination, is ugly and distressing in the extreme," he wrote after the Musehari experiment.

Soon after this came the change of mind of dozens of dreaded dacoits who were active in the Chambal valley. In October 1971, one of them, Madho Singh who had a price tag of Rs 1.5 lakh on his head visited JP at Patna and offered to surrender, provided society was willing to accept them. JP conferred with the Central and State governments and organised their surrender and rehabilitation. Between April 14 and 17 of 1972, nearly 200 of them surrendered before JP, with a picture of Gandhi in the background. "Until today we only met people who wanted to capture or kill us. You are the only person who wanted to save us," one of them wept before JP.

The year 1972 had more surprises in store for JP, unpleasant ones. In October, JP was undergoing treatment at Banaras Medical College and he suggested that Prabhavati undergo a routine medical check-up. It was rude shock when it was discovered that she had cancer of the ovary. She was taken to Bombay and operated upon, but recovery was elusive. On April 15, 1973, she breathed her last. JP realised how much the shadow that followed him through decades meant to him. "I cannot tell you what her absence means to me. There is no zest or interest left in life, and the very will to live seems to be dead within me. I continue to do my work, to the extent my health permits — as a matter of duty rather than as something that I enjoy or that gives me spiritual satisfaction," he wrote to a friend in Australia who wrote his biography later.

Meanwhile, the social and political situation in the country had moved from bad to worse. In the early 1970s, the country faced a severe economic crisis and this was amplified by the Bangladesh War of 1971. Corruption was rampant and power was being centralised more and more. JP's disenchantment with the failure of the Sarvodaya Movement convinced him that it was time for direct action — that meant *Satyagrahas* and demonstration — for an Indian social transformation. On the contrary, Vinoba held on to the opinion that in an independent democratic country such direct actions and Civil Disobedience were anachronistic. JP tried to persuade Vinoba but he said that his hearing was impaired and asked JP to tell his secretary Nirmala Deshpande what was his action plan. JP thought it was a deliberate attempt on Vinoba's part to humiliate him. In July 1974, at a conference of the Sarvodaya workers, JP finally parted ways with Vinoba Bhave, his spiritual guru for more that two decades.

Independent of JP and the Sarvodaya workers a new wave of political protest, largely initiated by students agitated over inflation, was taking shape against the Congress governments. Opposition parties swept over by Indira Gandhi's populist *garibi hatao* slogan in the 1971 general election regrouped around the student agitators. For the ideologically disparate opposition groups ranging from Naxals to the RSS, Jayaprakash Narayan became the common factor. From political wilderness of two decades, JP soon reinvented himself as Loknayak — Leader of the People.

CHAPTER FOUR

# The JP Movement

The country was in turmoil. The euphoria of independence that promised prosperity for all had long faded. Rising prices, unemployment, poverty and corruption increased. Hopelessness and unrest ruled the day. Gandhi was long gone; it was time for a new prophet. "The situation was ripe. ... I did recognise that a revolutionary situation had arisen and something had to be done," JP explained his decision to plunge into political action.

JP wanted to promote a viable opposition in the country that was under almost absolute Congress hegemony. But still he was wary about his role in such a move the beginning. In February 1973, Biju Patnaik of the Utkal Congress in Orissa approached JP with the proposal that he take up the leadership of an opposition confederation. JP turned down the offer, but offered "consultation and advice" for any such move. In July 1973, JP started *Everyman's,* an English weekly from Delhi, which he said was "not wedded to any isms — left, right or centre." This political neutrality, condensed later in the rather ambiguous slogan of 'Total Revolution' became the ideological fuel for the unified opposition agitation against the Congress.

It all started with the students of Gujarat hitting the roads, protesting the mess fees hike in December 1973. With opposition parties supporting the student agitators, the Gujarat Navanirman Samiti, was formed which expanded the scope of the agitation to address larger issues like corruption. The Samiti demanded the resignation of the State Government and the dissolution of the Assembly. JP visited Ahmedabad and exhorted the students to "put moral pressure" on MLAs to resign. At the end of several *bandhs* and widespread violence, Chief Minister Chimanbhai Patel resigned on February 9, 1974 and the Assembly was dissolved later. JP saw in the Gujarat agitation an explicit expression of what he thought was a revolutionary situation. "There is another 1942 Movement in sight to change the course of history," JP declared.

*A cartoon by O V Vijayan*

*JP coming to address a public meeting in Gandhi Maidan, Patna*

*Surrounded by journalists in Patna on the eve of the Patna demonstration in April, 1974*

Encouraged by the success in Gujarat, students in Bihar also began a movement which initially was one for fee reduction and more employment opportunities. Started in early 1974, that snowballed into the largest popular mobilisation independent India had seen until then. On March 18, 1974 more than 10,000 students laid siege to the Bihar Assembly. The procession was allegedly infiltrated by outside elements causing considerable violence. The student leaders were consulting JP on their struggle. Immediately after he heard about the violence, JP summoned them. "He asked us specific questions about violence at particular places. Once convinced that we did not cause violence, he stood by us," recalls Ram Bahadur Rai, one of the leaders then. Still JP did not come out openly in their support. The students continued with their struggle which had now become one "against corruption". On April 12, 1974, at Gaya, police fired at a rally killing eight and injuring twelve. This agitated JP no end and he took the leadership of the struggle while addressing a rally of nearly two lakh people in Gaya on April 16 since things were "now beyond tolerance." "Without JP joining the agitation, the movement would not have survived any longer," says Rai. What began as a student agitation suddenly became a mass movement in which not only opposition parties, but many other voluntary organisations and even the RSS and the Anand Marg actively participated.

JP organised Citizens for Democracy, in Delhi in April 1974 aimed to "preserve and strengthen democracy," which he perceived was being seriously challenged by the centralised administrative system. Towards the end of the month he left for Vellore in Tamil Nadu for a prostrate operation. By the time he returned to the battlefield in June, Bihar was boiling, with the Chhatra Sangarsh Samiti (the students struggle committee) having effectively kept the fire burning. With

*JP joins the movement. Kumar Prasad, editor of 'Tarun Kranti' ties the inaugural scarf round the leader's neck*

the effective intervention of JP the struggle was now expanding beyond students and included electoral reforms and accountability of administrators in its demands. JP maintained that the Bihar Government and its legislators did not enjoy the support of the people and hence should resign. On June 5, JP led five lakh people to the Raj Bhawan — the governor's residence — with signatures of lakhs more, demanding the resignation of the ministry.

On the face of criticism that he was using pressure tactics to remove an elected government rather than wait till the next elections, JP justified the agitation on the ground that there was no legal provision of recalling legislatures. JP involved political parties in the agitation through Jan Sangarsh Samitis and an 11-member steering committee was formed to organise the agitation. JP consulted each one individually and then the committee, but quite often did what he thought was right. "I will take the advice of all, of the students, the people, the Jan Sangarsh

*Crowds gathered in millions wherever JP spoke*

Samitis. But the decision will be mine and you will have to accept them," JP said as a precondition for taking up the leadership of the struggle. The government responded with repressive measures. By July 1, there were 1600 people in jail. In August, JP raised the pitch by calling for a no-tax campaign. On August 15 that year, agitators organised Peoples' Independence Day in contrast to the state organised celebrations. On October 3, 4 and 5, a three-day *bandh* was organised across Bihar.

With every rally, JP was attracting a bigger crowd in Bihar and he expanded his campaign to other States as well. He went to Uttar Pradesh, Haryana, Rajasthan and Punjab. By early 1975, JP explained his movement as one for 'Total Revolution' *ie,* "radical, social, economical, political, educational, cultural and ethical change." He was always at pains to explain to his followers that not *satta parivartan* (change in government), but *vyavastha parivartan* (change in the system) was the goal and aim of his movement. "Our aim is not to replace the Congress with BJD or Jan Sangh," JP repeatedly reiterated. In every youth meeting that JP addressed, he exhorted them to break off the sacred thread and take a vow for a dowry-less marriage, to bring about social change that is not enforced by the State. In every town that he went, there were three meetings — students and youth, political leaders and then intellectuals and writers. JP explained his concepts, which sounded everything for everybody and attracted large following in a desperate country. Still 'Total Revolution', by JP's own admission, did not have any specific economic programme. "The vagueness of the concept 'Total Revolution' was a calculated move to keep conflicting interests together," feels Arif Mohammad Khan, who was a key student leader in the agitation. The movement grew in leaps and bounds.

*JP's declaration before being admitted to Jaslok Hospital*

Referring to his demands for dissolution of the Assembly, Prime Minister Indira Gandhi said he was undermining the democratic institutions. JP retorted that she had already undermined the judiciary and was concentrating all powers in the executive. On November 4, the police cracked down heavily on a rally organised in Patna. Later the same month, he responded to Indira Gandhi's suggestion that the agitators should wait till the next elections. "I take up her challenge. ... You have made me the Nayak of this agitation. I shall also be your Nayak in the elections," JP told a rally on November 18. On the November 25, he attended a coordination committee meeting of opposition parties in Delhi and insisted that they should field common candidates against the Congress in the next elections. By March 1975, the venue of the struggle had been shifted to Delhi with a massive rally on the 6th of the month. By this time, the immediate political aim of the movement was unseating the Indira Government, quite far from the grandiose theme of 'Total Revolution'.

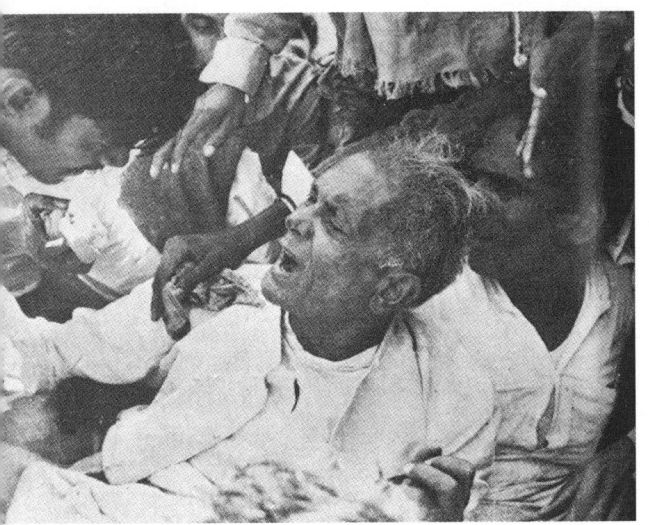

*The lathi-blow that rocked India. JP being carried after he had been felled by a policeman. He was saved from serious injury by his followers, who took the initial impact*

Removing Indira was no easy task. But JP's Movement got a fillip with the Allahabad High Court verdict of June 12, 1975 invalidating Indira Gandhi's 1971 election from the Rai Bareilly constituency. Indira Gandhi refused to resign. On June 25, 1975, Opposition parties organised a huge rally in Delhi addressed by JP, Morarji Desai and others. The rally signalled a campaign of *Satyagraha* to gain the desired result. In the rally, JP repeated his plea to the

*The Tea Party: JP with Congress Members of Parliament at the residence of K. Chandrasekhar, November 20 1974*

army and police to disobey what he thought was illegal orders of the government, which he had been describing as of "usurpers". Indira Gandhi used this as an excuse and clamped Internal Emergency by the midnight of June 25-26 , 1975. JP, who was resting at the Gandhi Peace Foundation in Delhi received the midnight knock of police, as did virtually all other opposition leaders in the country. India woke to the silent morning of 26th, devoid of protest slogans and political demands. Democracy was interrupted in India.

After his arrest, JP was kept in solitary confinement in the Chandigarh Medical Institute. While under arrest in Chandigarh during the Emergency days, JP wrote his prison diary, a detailed account of his dreams and disappointments about India. Against the backdrop of the Emergency declaration, JP's first entry on July 21, 1975, began on a note of despair and perhaps even a willingness to give up. "My world lies in shambles all around me," he wrote. "I am afraid, I shall not see it put together again in my lifetime. Here was I trying to widen the horizons of democracy and here am I ending up with the death of democracy?" In later pages, JP went on to elaborate his vision for the country, which he thought needed another liberation. The diary was published even while the censorship was on, and some of JP's friends believe that A.B. Shah who edited the book overdid his job, taking the sting out of it. Copies of the diary were auctioned — some at Rs 2000 — to raise funds for the Janata Party, the newly formed political party that took on the Congress might in 1977.

While in Chandigarh PGI, JP's health showed signs of failing. Trouble was with his kidney's and the delay in medical attention almost killed him. In fact many of his followers believed that JP's health was deliberately neglected and when the Janata Government came to power a commission was appointed to look into it. Then the health minister claimed that there were "shocking revelations" in the inquiry committee reports, but nothing was ultimately publicised. With his health deteriorating, the government agreed to release him on November 15, 1975. He was brought to AIIMS in a very critical condition and then taken to Jaslok Hospital in Mumbai. From January 1976, he had to be on regular dialysis till the end came.

Though bound to the dialysis machine, it did not deter JP from finishing the task he had assigned himself. Right out of the blue, on January 18, 1977, Indira Gandhi announced the dissolution of the Lok Sabha and general elections. JP persuaded the opposition parties — the Congress (O), Jan Sangh and the Bharatiya Lok Dal and socialist groups — to merge and form the Janata Party. JP set on a whirlwind campaign for the Janata Party. JP told the huge gatherings at his public meetings that the impending elections would decide the fate of India — to be democratic or to be under dictatorship. Every second day of his election programme was marked D, meaning dialysis. Fortunately JP's efforts were not an exercise in futility.

*March 24, 1977: Janata Party Members of Parliament being administered pledge by JP at Rajghat before taking office. Left to Right: Biju Patnaik, Mani Ram Baghri, JP (seated), N. Sanjiva Reddy, Jagjivan Ram, Morarji Desai, Maniben Patel and Acharya J.B. Kripalini (seated).*

On March 22, 1977, for the first time, after being in power for 25 years, the Congress Party was to surrender power as it was defeated in the general elections. Newspapers screamed headlines such as "Exit Indira" and "JP's role bigger than Gandhi's" even as the Janata wave swept away the high hopes of Indira Gandhi. JP was in Patna at the time of the announcement and the victorious MPs requested him to come to the Capital immediately. JP and Acharya Kripalini were entrusted with the task of electing the leader of the Janata Parliamentary Party — at the end of an agonising night, they declared Morarji Desai as the Prime Minister. On his 75th birthday, on October 11, 1977, JP said, "my life's work is over." But for his towering personality, as he had by then acquired the moral authority of a patron saint in opposition politics in the country, a coalition against Indira would have been just impossible. After the Janata Government

*March 23, 1977: Morarji Desai calls on J.P.*

came to power, Mulk Raj Anand, wrote to JP, "But for your magnanimity in forgetting the misdeeds of some constituents of the Janata Party (like the RSS suspected for backing the murderers of Gandhiji), the new combination may not have come to be."

In his last days, JP was a disappointed man. The movement had instilled a new life into JP who had become pessimistic after Prabhavati's death. JP was in a hurry. Once the Janata Government came to power, he felt there was now no goal to pursue. He retired to Patna's Kadam Kuan locality where he had acquired a small house in the 1950s. He stayed in the first floor of the double storeyed building which had an air conditioner, a bed and two chairs.

Attached to him was the indispensable dialysis machine. From the ground floor, his secretaries Abraham and Sachidanand functioned, sorting out hundreds of letters that he received every day. Most of those letters sought JP's intervention with the Central Government on some issue or the other. But many of JP's recommendations were not accepted by the Desai government and this led to speculations that a rift had developed between JP and his protégé' in the government. What JP said by way of explanation sounded more like a statement of helplessness than detachment, "I have no grievance that the Janata government doesn't consult me. I am neither a member of the party, nor do I hold any office. How can I, a private citizen, wish that the government should consult me on all matters?"

Soon after the dialysis, he felt youthful freshness and carried on his work with vigour and met a large number of people, recalls Anand Kumar, teacher at Jawaharlal Nehru University, who spent a lot of time with JP during his last days. Kumar was among the student leaders of the early 1970s. In the initial days of the Janata Government, JP refused to comment on its performance. He had vowed silence on the issue for one year and later extended it for another six months. JP broke that silence in an interview with Anand Kumar. JP said he was happy that there was no extra-constitutional authority; ministers were rather modest in their lifestyles and behaviour. But he wrote in a letter drafted by Kumar to Chandrashekhar and Moraji Desai that it (the government) was an opportunity and warned that they should not go the Congress way.

Away from the petty squabbling of his usurped disciples in Delhi, where according to JP, Gandhi lay buried in more than one sense, JP died a lonely death on October 8, 1979, just three days before his 77th birthday. With his death ended a political episode that spanned six decades, survived and defeated governments before and after the end of colonialism. Jayaprakash Narayan had been called a saint, rebel and revolutionary in different moments of Indian history.

CHAPTER FIVE

# The Man and His Ideas

JP who was tall and handsome; during his student days in the United States, was a delightful distraction to several of his female classmates. Later on in life, he wore half-rimmed spectacles and his slightly protruding lower lips were to become the cartoonists' delight, who never lost the opportunity to scoff at his highly idealistic world view. JP was conscious of his appearance — he carried a comb and before he stood for a public address, he combed his receding hair. When abroad, he wore sober suits, within India, freshly starched *kurta* and *dhoti* or *pyjama*. After his wife's death in 1973, he seemed less interested in looking good. He did not make a show of poverty — he travelled first class whenever necessary.

Prabhavati was a constant presence in JP's life, bringing in some order into an otherwise chaotic lifestyle. JP was unpunctual — he kept people waiting for hours at times. He was forgetful — he would call people for dinner and forget it. He was incapable of handling money — such that even before he boarded a train, the money for the trip would be exhausted. JP and Prabha adopted a daughter, Janaki, who was married to Kumar Prashant, a Sarvodaya worker. JP ever the idealist, jumped from one dream to another.

At times JP was confused in many of his public pronouncements and actions, enabling his opponents to question his consistency. He was childlike, modest and humanity was the centre of his thinking and activities. JP exaggerated his capability and moral authority, like Gandhi did, and declared superhuman objectives for many of his movements which would soon be inflicted with intrigues and politicking. From the Socialist days to the Janata experiment, this holds true. For instance the Bihar movement, by JP's own admission, became merely one for the removal of the government. But "unlike Gandhi, he was somewhat naïve in his judgement of men."

He spoke and wrote Hindi and English well and even Bhojpuri. JP was not a great orator; he spoke like a teacher who tutors little children and at times exceedingly boringly. But when ignited by passion, he struck a cord with the huge crowds that he invariably attracted because his sincerity and intentions were always above board.

When JP and Minoo Masani, JP's Socialist colleague and later Swatantra Party leader, used to call on Gandhi in the 1930s, Masani would do a *namaste,* but JP would invariably bend down and touch Gandhi's feet. Asked whether it was not contradictory to his Marxian beliefs, JP said, he had been brought up like a good Hindu and hence showing respect to elders was part of his upbringing. Moreover his loyalty to Marxism was not sufficient for him to join the Marxist Party at the time of his return from the US. He was a nationalist first and foremost and joined the National movement.

*JP with M.R. Masani*

JP was a staunch advocate of individual freedom — though in earlier his days, in defence of the Soviet experience he had said that, for a hungry man voting rights mean nothing. Once he felt that individual freedom faced a threat from the state machinery, JP roared into action with a passion that was rarely reflected in his earlier life. "Freedom has become a passion for life, and I shall not see it compromised for bread, for power, for security, for prosperity, for the glory of the state or for anything else," JP said after his rejection of Marxism.

Though a votary of public democracy, JP was often unilateral in his organisational functioning. J.B. Kripalini writes that it was JP's habit of taking important decisions without consultation since the socialist days, irritating his colleagues, most notably Rammanohar Lohia. On economic affairs and the mode of development, JP changed his views too often; during the last movement he even said it was not desirable to have a clear-cut economic programme for a movement like his.

For JP, opposition was never personal and his concern was about people in distress. After her defeat in the 1977 elections, JP had a one hour talk with Indira Gandhi. Several times, the top position in the country was within reach but his natural inclination was to run away from power, and he trusted others implicitly, making him a misfit for conventional politics.

In 1936, JP's pamphlet "Why Socialism" examined the concept of Socialism and argued that taking control of the state apparatus was necessary for bringing about socialism. JP was

*An old revolutionary makes peace in troubled Nagaland*

mildly critical of the Russian model of development and administration — it was already in place — but could not overlook the strides of progress it was making. Those days JP was an avowed modernist and his views on development were diametrically opposite to what he would say or do three decades later. He was not a votary of autonomous village units then. JP wanted them to be "progressive communities, connected to the rest of the world with electricity, railways, telephones, radios, roads, buses. The village too will become an industrial unit of production like the city." He also attacked Gandhi's ideas of "class collaboration," trusteeship and non-violence.

Campaigning for the 1952 elections for the Socialist Party, he lost faith in the Westminster model parliamentary system. He felt it leads to impossible promises and manipulation of an

*Addressing a public meeting in pouring rain at Allahabad, June 1974*

illiterate and poverty-stricken electorate. JP thought parliamentary democracy was biased against the poor, who were to be influenced by the unethical influence of big money in politics. Around the same time he lost faith also in welfare system which was at the "mercy of a remote elite" and communist state-oriented development which was showing its authoritarian tendencies in the USSR. But JP maintained throughout his life that parliamentary democracy should be made successful until a better form, which he called 'party-less' democracy could be achieved.

The concept of 'party-less' emerged during the *Bhudan* years. JP suggested that as a beginning, parties keep away from local body elections. Also, he suggested, a delegation of voters select candidates for general elections rather than individual political parties. Kripalini had suggested to him to form a Gandhian political party by the late 1950s, but JP toyed with the idea of party-less democracy until 1975, when he virtually accepted parties.

By late 1950s, he had been convinced that socialism cannot be a state project. His goal was to create and develop forms of socialist living through the voluntary endeavour of the people rather than seek to "establish socialism by the use of power of the state." "Our means must be pure and fair, because our ends are fair," JP the Gandhian proclaimed.

JP turned a critic of the Welfare State and interpreted Gandhi to say that "the government that governs the least is the best government." This position of JP took him closer to the conservatives in the Indian political spectrum rather than the interventionists. JP who refused to join the Nehru cabinet because the latter refused to nationalise banks, said after Indira Gandhi nationalised them that "nationalisation has not achieved anything for socialism in our country except a transfer of private ownership to state ownership."

At every given point, JP was so sure about his ideology that he did not let anyone question him, other than his experiences. And when experiences did disappoint him, which was not rare, JP made amends and moved on. From Marxism to Gandhism and Sarvodaya-Bhudan to Total Revolution, JP made demigods of his contemporary belief systems. Gandhi was a reactionary for JP in the 1930s, but after committing himself to Gandhism, he regretted why he did not do it earlier. Minoo Masani asked JP to read *Assignment In Utopia*, a book that unmasked socialist USSR, but JP refused, because he did not want his impressions about the USSR to be dashed. His good relations with Vinoba, which began from the change of heart he instilled in the landlord of Telangana waned gradually.

During his *Bhudan* years, JP who was earlier an admirer of Soviet Planning, opposed the constitution of the Planning Commission. "Difference between the socialism that is in fashion and Gandhiji's socialism, which he preferred to call *sarvodaya*, is that for him socialism or rather *sarvodaya*, began from the bottom. *sarvodaya* begins from *antyodaya* (the rise of the last and the lowliest) he used to emphasise" said JP. His rural centric work included helping peasantry get better seed, build small irrigation projects and improve housing facilities. He firmly believed in decentralisation so that even the smallest unit in the polity had a say in their development. His split with Vinoba was because of the varying approaches that they both conceived for solving the problems. Vinoba wanted to wait for *lok shakti* — people's power which he thought was the source of all social reformation — to ripen, JP thought students of Gujarat and Bihar had already taken to streets and there was nothing more to wait for in 1974.

His encounter with the Naxalites earlier was an eye-opener for JP. During his stay in Muzaffarpur in Bihar, where Naxalites had threatened to kill two Sarvodaya workers in 1972, he engaged himself in consolidating declared *gramdans*, and in the process discovered the actual conditions of typical Indian villages. His impressions, experiences and ideas came out as a booklet of 28 pages, *Face to Face*. He realised that Vinobaji's method of preaching and persuading was not adequate in the given condition. "Condition seems to be ripening in the context of our present programme that may necessitate large-scale *satyagraha*." Later on, not only did Vinobaji disapprove of the Bihar students' movement which JP had agreed to lead, but also started making mild yet adverse remarks about it.

In 'Total Revolution', which was the mascot for the 1974 JP Movement, more than economic disparities, social ones were considered more pernicious. So addressing issues like casteism and dowry became the campaign points for JP personally, whereas for most of his colleagues who were peeved with Indira Gandhi's state socialist policies, JP's stance on a non-interventionist state was the attraction. JP too balanced his pronouncements to keep the conservatives and radicals happy at the same time. Addressing a meeting of trade unions in Mumbai he said, capitalists in the country never had it so good as under Indira Gandhi. In the same breath, he would say state planning had led to retarding of production.

He thought democracy must be all pervasive. JP believed there should be measures for population control through education and persuasion. He thought India's elections were not representative of people's opinion which stemmed from his knowledge of the unpopularity of the Congress leaders and his anxiety to make Indian elections fair and free — electoral reforms became a major demand of the 1974 Movement. For himself JP never sought a seat in legislature. He had said, once the Janata government came to power, that it also should be

With Willy Brandt in Berlin

criticised with the same vehemence as the Congress was being criticised.

JP's critique of the Indian administrative system in the early 1970s is well-summed up in a letter that he wrote to the leaders of the newly formed Bangladesh, a cause supported by JP. He asked them to learn "from the experience of India," where leaders had occupied palatial bungalows vacated by their earlier colonisers. "The result has been not only waste of much public money but also the estrangement between the rulers and the ruled."

He advised the Bangladeshis against adopting the Indian administrative model, which he said was "outmoded, rule-bound and procedure-clogged and is more or less the same as the British had left behind." In the same letter, he wrote that the public sector units in India which had an investment of 4000 crore had an annual return of less than one percent, "a wasteful luxury" that Bangladesh can "hardly afford."

His *Prison Diary* reveals his spiritual pilgrimage with anguish and anxiety as to how India was to plan her future. It was both about action and meditation. He believed the elected have no right to continue in office if their electors did not wish so, irrespective of their remaining legal term. JP always retained his power to see things above and beyond electoral politics. After the Congress was defeated, JP was asked what his biggest achievement was and what remained to be sought. "The most important achievement for which I cannot take the entire credit is the unprecedented mass awakening, particularly the awakening among the youth. The task that

*Receiving the Magsaysay Award from the Philippines President Macapagal, 1965*

remains to be done is to win the resurgent people's and youth power for changing constructively Indian society in its entirety."

Jayaprakash Narayan, the Lok Nayak was admired far beyond Indian boundaries. While in the US in May 1977 for treatment, Jimmy Carter wrote to JP, "Your devotion to freedom and democracy has inspired us all." The Magsaysay Award citation 1965, described him as the "keeper of the conscience of a people." Perhaps, in his death, the nation lost its conscience too.

## Select Bibliography

Lakshmi Narayan Lal, *Jayaprakash: Rebel Extraordinary*
Indian Books, New Delhi, 1975

Ajit Bhattacharjea, *Jayaprakash Narayan: A Political Biography*
Vikas, Delhi, 1975

K L Sharma (Ed), *Jayaprakash Narayan: Abhinanthan Granth*
Chinmaya Publications, Jaipur, 1978

Bimal Prasad, *Jayaprakash Narayan: Quest and Legacy*
Vikas, New Delhi, 1992

Allan Scarfe and Wendy Scarfe, *JP: His Biography*
Orient Longman, New Delhi 1975

Minoo Masani, *JP: Mission Partly Accomplished*
Macmillan, Delhi, 1977